Redemptive Suffering

Redemptive Suffering

Offering Ourselves with Jesus to the Father
for the Salvation of Mankind

Fr. Samuel Tiesi, T.O.R.

FRANCISCAN UNIVERSITY PRESS
Franciscan University of Steubenville
Steubenville, OH 43952

©1995 by Fr. Samuel Tiesi, T.O.R. All rights reserved

Printed in the United States of America

1995 Publication by:
Franciscan University Press
Franciscan University of Steubenville
Steubenville, Ohio 43952

Cover Art and Design: © by Dawn C. Harris
Cover Photo: © by Raymond Recznik

ISBN–940535–86–6

UP–186

To our Lady of Sorrows, Co-Redemptrix of mankind. I ask her to teach us how to share in the sufferings of Christ by uniting us to her Immaculate Heart and the Sacred Heart of Jesus, thus converting our daily suffering into redemptive suffering.

Whoever remains in me and I in him will bear much fruit, because without me you can do nothing. . . . If you remain in me and my words remain in you, ask for whatever you want and it will be done for you. By this is my Father glorified, that you bear much fruit and become my disciples. As the Father loves me, so I also love you. Remain in my love. If you keep my commandments, you will remain in my love, just as I have kept my Father's commandments and remain in his love.

(John 15:5, 7–10 NABrNT)

Contents

Foreword

This is a powerful proclamation on the place of human suffering in the Christian life. It is filled with hope and will inspire any serious disciple of the Lord to honor suffering in a new way. It is written by a Franciscan friar and priest whose ministry is to the ill and elderly of our own Franciscan T.O.R. community.

My brother Father Sam and I have been together for most of our lives. We lived together in the same house for about twenty-five years, and during our other years of apostolic service we have regularly interacted. Sam is as sincere and heartfelt a speaker as I have ever known. He writes the same way. He teaches redemptive suffering in this booklet with directness and insight acquired from his own experience and profound reflection on the Word of God. It is not just theory but theology in its basic sense that the practice or action for God is reflected on and explained.

We all have the opportunity for redemptive suffering, for indeed we all will suffer. If we know God, we can convert this suffering into redemptive value. But beyond this, as the saints teach us, the suffering itself brings forth joy. It is all here in direct, simple language suited for the person suffering or the one reflecting on the sufferings of others.

In First Peter we read that we should "always be prepared to give an explanation for the hope that is in you" (3:15). The power of such a witness varies according to the intensity of the suffering and the spiritual depth of the joy manifested. It is only redemptive suffering that gives an explanation for such joy, and Sam shows that we can do it.

Fr. Michael Scanlan, T.O.R.

Introduction

The purpose of this little book is to help rekindle the desire among Christians to accept and practice a forgotten yet very important doctrine of our faith, namely redemptive suffering. Although Jesus Christ fully redeemed mankind by his passion and death, we are still called to share in that redemptive action. The Canon of the Mass tells us that Christ died to make of us an offering to God. As St. Paul said: "in my flesh I complete what is lacking in Christ's afflictions for the sake of his body, that is, the church" (Colossians 1:24).

In many cases it is possible to relieve physical and psychological suffering, but sometimes we become impatient to relieve it. We do not even consider that there is great value and merit in believing and accepting that suffering is used by God to discipline, purify, justify, and sanctify us—and others through us. With this sanctification through suffering comes the only true joy that we can experience on earth. This is because suffering is part of the mystery of love.

What has motivated me from start to finish in writing this little book is the knowledge that many Christians do not know the value of suffering, and thus much of their suffering "goes to waste" and is not converted into redemptive suffering. My hope is that at least those who know me will take the time to read this and thus become more united to Christ, the Crucified One.

As you read *Redemptive Suffering,* I hope your desire to share in the suffering of Christ grows as much as my desire to participate in the passion and death of Christ grew while I was writing it. Please read it prayerfully.

1

"Behold, I Make All Things New" (Revelation 21:5)

On October 11, 1961, Pope John XXIII prayed for a "New Pentecost" as he convoked the Second Vatican Council. I believe that we have been experiencing a new Pentecost through all the Spirit-filled movements of our age. The Holy Spirit of God desires to renew belief in all our Christian truths. The truths themselves are as beautiful as ever but they do not appear so to modern, jaded minds. Slowly but surely the Spirit of God is once again going to permeate us and bring to life for us all those doctrines, traditions, and devotions which were first enunciated by the Holy Spirit himself. Here are just a few of the teachings that I perceive God emphasizing in our age so they and we will "come alive" together.

First, *God wants us to know that he is our Father.* He created us and we belong to him. He is in the process of recreating us in his image and likeness, that is, into being his perfected children. How wonderful it is to know that the Almighty, All-Knowing, and All-Loving God is indeed our Father. It is Jesus, the only begotten Son of the Father who taught us this truth when he said: "Go to my brethren and say to them, I am ascending to my Father and your Father, to my God and your God" (John 20:17).

Second, *God is reminding us that he is Love* and loves us so much that he sent his Son into the world to save us from sin and death. We did not deserve or merit this; it is a manifestation of his mercy. He sees us in our misery and shows us his merciful love. Yes, "God so loved the world that he gave his only Son, that whoever believes in him should not perish but have eternal life" (John 3:16). Jesus instructs us, "Be merciful even as your Father is merciful" (Luke 6:36).

Third, *Jesus Christ is still with us in a very special way in the Holy Sacrifice of the Mass.* The Eucharist is the Body and Blood, Soul and Divinity of our Lord and Savior

Jesus Christ. Jesus so loved the world that he invented this Sacrament of Love so that he could go to the Father and still remain with us. He decided to remain with us in this sacramental, sacrificial way and he wants to be adored as our Eucharistic Lord. Jesus, Emmanuel (*God with us*), is still with us in the Blessed Sacrament. Jesus, the Lamb of God, is still with us as the sacrificial lamb in the Holy Sacrifice of the Mass. And Jesus, the Bread of Life, is still with us as bread from heaven in Holy Communion.

Fourth, *he wants us to take more seriously the doctrine of the indwelling of the Blessed Trinity.* Jesus says, "If a man loves me, he will keep my word, and my Father will love him, and we will come to him and make our home with him" (John 14:23). Each of our bodies is a "temple of the Holy Spirit" (1 Corinthians 6:19). Yes, it is the true God—the Father, Son, and Holy Spirit—who dwells within us. The whole Trinitarian action of the Father, Son, and Spirit is taking place in our souls. Jesus is constantly offering himself to Abba Father in the Holy Spirit. Jesus is constantly revealing the Father to us with his Spirit-filled words. We need to probe more deeply into this fundamental doctrine of our faith.

Fifth, *Jesus wants us to acknowledge the Virgin Mary as his most Blessed Mother* who played and is playing a unique, major role in the history of our salvation. He wants us to give her the honor and praise that is her due as mother of Christ the Redeemer. We need to know that because we are the Body of Christ, she is the mother of us all. "Jesus . . . said to his mother, 'Woman, behold, your son!' Then he said to the disciple, 'Behold, your mother!'" (John 19:25–26). God wants Mary to do as much for us as she did for Jesus. I believe that just as the Holy Spirit and Mary brought us Jesus, the firstborn of many, so too the Holy Spirit and Mary are forming us into being brothers and sisters of Jesus. I believe that she will not stop until all mankind has become one with Jesus.

Finally, *God wants us, in some mysterious way, to share intimately in the redemptive action of Jesus Christ.* He wants us to do just what St. Paul did: "Now I rejoice in my sufferings for your sake, and in my flesh I complete what is lacking in Christ's afflictions for the sake of his body, that is, the church" (Colossians 1:24). We too must fill up in our flesh the sufferings that God the Father wills for us for the sake of the salvation of mankind. We must humble ourselves before the Lord to accept the lot chosen for us. And the actions and desires of St. Paul we should make our own: "For his sake I have suffered the loss of all things . . . that I may know him and the power of his resurrection, and may share his sufferings, becoming like him in his death, that if possible I may attain the resurrection from the dead" (Philippians 3:8, 10–11).

Jesus, our leader, suffered and died before rising and ascending into glory. St. Paul lived in imitation of Christ and encourages us to have the same attitude: "Have his mind among yourselves, which was in Christ Jesus, who, though he was in the form of God, did not count equality with God a thing to be grasped, but emptied himself, taking the form of a servant, being born in the likeness of men. And being found in human form he humbled himself and became obedient unto death, even death on a cross" (Philippians 2:5–8).

We who are baptized and are in the state of sanctifying grace make up the Mystical Body of Christ. We are an extension of Christ in time and space. Not only must the head suffer, die, and rise in order to enter into glory but the whole body of Christ must do the same because that is the plan of the Father. I like to look at it this way. Jesus offered himself to the Father. He was both priest and victim. And in Jesus' offer of himself to the Father, we, his Mystical Body, were also offered. We were incorporated into his Body at our Baptism. Will we suffer along with him? Will we offer that suffering to the Father along with him? He awaits our response. We are to say *yes* and let him offer us. Our greatest call is to become one with Christ who is both priest and victim, to offer ourselves as a "living sacrifice with him" (Romans 12) to the Father. "Be imitators of God, as beloved children. And walk in love, as Christ loved us and gave himself up for us, a fragrant offering and sacrifice to God" (Ephesians 5:1–2).

Jesus Christ came on a mission. His mission was to redeem mankind. He gave himself as a ransom to free us from the kingdom of darkness. "Lord, by your cross and resurrection, you have set us free" (acclamation from the Third Canon of the Mass). By his action he gave us the freedom to choose whether or not to follow him. Every true follower of Jesus has been co-missioned to share in the redemptive action of Jesus Christ, the King of kings and Lord of lords.

2

Creation Story

When considering suffering, death, and resurrection it is necessary to go back to the creation story in the Bible: "The Lord then took the man and settled him in the garden of Eden, to cultivate and care for it. The Lord God gave man this order: 'You are free to eat from any of the trees of the garden except the tree of knowledge of good and bad, from that tree you shall not eat. The moment you eat from it you are surely doomed to die'" (Genesis 2:15–17).

It is all history now. Adam and Eve ate of the forbidden fruit, i.e., they sinned and were thereby doomed to die. It seems that suffering and death are the direct consequences of sin. St. Paul calls death "the wages of sin" (Romans 6:23). Justice demands that we render to another his due. Death is due the sinner. Since our first parents were sinners, all their children were born in sin. I like to look at it this way: Like breeds like. Adam and Eve had to give birth to their kind. St. Paul explains the fall and our redemption thus: "As one man's trespass led to condemnation for all men, so one man's act of righteousness leads to acquittal and life for all men. For as by one man's disobedience many were made sinners, so by one man's obedience many will be made righteous" (Romans 5:18–19).

The process of Jesus making all things right between God and man is the story of our salvation. It is the story of how Jesus saved us from our miserable state of eternal death by offering himself in sacrifice to Abba, Father. Jesus redeemed us by suffering and dying on the cross. He poured out his precious blood for us.

When the Son of God decided to take to himself our human condition, it was one that was depraved and living under the consequences of Original Sin. Jesus was obedient unto death, even death on the cross. His Father did not save him from dying, but from Death, by raising him up on the third day.

In the days of his flesh, Jesus offered up prayers and supplications, with loud cries and tears, to him who was able to save him from death, and he was heard for his godly fear. Although he was a Son, he learned obedience through what he suffered; and being made perfect he became the source of eternal salvation to all who obey him, being designated by God a high priest after the order of Melchizedek. (Hebrews 5:7–10)

The story of Jesus and two disciples on the road to Emmaus is a moving account of Jesus' redemptive action leading to his glorious triumph over death:

And he said to them, "What is this conversation which you are holding with each other as you walk?" And they stood still, looking sad. Then one of them, named Cleopas, answered him, "Are you the only visitor to Jerusalem who does not know the things that have happened there in these days?" And he said to them,

"What things?" And they said to him, "Concerning Jesus of Nazareth, who was a prophet mighty in deed and word before God and all the people, and how our chief priests and rulers delivered him up to be condemned to death, and crucified him. But we had hoped that he was the one to redeem Israel. Yes, and besides all this, it is now the third day since this happened. Moreover, some women of our company amazed us. They were at the tomb early in the morning and did not find his body; and they came back saying that they had even seen a vision of angels, who said that he was alive. Some of those who were with us went to the tomb, and found it just as the women had said; but him they did not see." And he said to them, "O foolish men, and slow of heart to believe all that the prophets have spoken! Was it not necessary that the Christ should suffer these things and enter into his glory?" (Luke 24:17–26)

Later that same day Jesus appeared to the apostles and explained further about redemptive suffering:

> Then he opened their minds to understand the scriptures, and said to them, "Thus it is written, that the Christ should suffer and on the third day rise from the dead, and that repentance and forgiveness of sins should be preached in his name to all nations, beginning from Jerusalem." (Luke 24:45–47)

3

We Too Must Suffer

Jesus suffered and died for us. Many Christians have been deceived down through the ages into believing that since Jesus suffered and died for us we no longer have to suffer and die. They think that there is no meaning for us in the cross and that his glory is already our glory. Oh, we of little sense! Do we not know that if Jesus and his mother, God the Father's favorites, had to suffer and die in order to enter into glory, we his followers have to do the same in order to enter into glory? "If we die with him we shall rise with him." We too must travel the "narrow road" and take up our crosses daily.

No one teaches the mystical body of Christ and the theology of suffering better than St. Paul. From his writings we can deduce that just as the head of the body suffered, died, and rose again so does the whole Mystical Body have to suffer, die, and rise to enter into glory. We must embrace our crosses. Padre Pio reportedly said that if we knew the value of suffering we would long for it. The saints understood the value of suffering so much that it sometimes brought them intense joy to suffer. Through redemptive suffering we become united with him who is perfect Truth, Beauty, and Goodness. It is the process whereby we become perfect lovers and shed those defects that attach us to ourselves or other created persons or things rather than to God. Suffering can bring true joy.

Jesus offered himself. He is priest and victim. Each of us is to be both priest and victim, offering ourselves along with Christ Jesus to the Father. Mary, the mother of Jesus, did it this way. She offered Jesus in the temple as a baby, at which time Simeon prophesied that a sword would pierce her heart (cf. Luke 2:35). She was there at the foot of the cross when Jesus said, "It is finished" (John 19:30) and "Father, into thy hands I commit my spirit!" (Luke 23:46). Mary was there suffering with him, offering with him. We were included in the offerings Jesus made to the Father. He offered his whole body. We are included in the offering of Mary for she offered his whole Mystical Body along with her own sufferings at the foot of the cross. And just as Mary, his mother, suffered with him to the end, we can trust that Mary, our mother, will suffer with us until the end.

4

The Holy Sacrifice of the Mass

What we have just said about Jesus' sacrifice on the cross we can also say about the Holy Sacrifice of the Mass. The Holy Sacrifice of the Mass is the passion and death of Jesus perpetuated. The following words from Pope John Paul II's letter "The Mystery and Worship of the Holy Eucharist" *(Dominicae Cenae),* February 24, 1980, speak clearly:

The eucharist is above all else a sacrifice. It is the sacrifice of the redemption and also the sacrifice of the new covenant, as we believe and as the Eastern churches clearly profess: "Today's sacrifice," the Greek church stated centuries ago, "is like that offered once by the only-begotten incarnate word: it is offered by him (now as then), since it is one and the same sacrifice." Accordingly, precisely by making this single sacrifice

21

of our salvation present, man and the world are restored to God through the paschal newness of redemption. This restoration cannot cease to be: It is the foundation of the "new and eternal covenant" of God with man and of man with God. If it were missing, one would have to question both the excellence of the sacrifice of the redemption, which in fact was perfect and definitive, and also the sacrificial value of the Mass. In fact, the eucharist, being a true sacrifice, brings about this restoration to God.[1]

Jesus, therefore, remains with us in the sacrificial form and we remain with him in sacrifice. In Romans, Chapter 12, we are told to offer our bodies as a living sacrifice to God. Every aspect of our lives must be offered to God. Our goal is to love Christ Jesus by becoming one with him. It is to become one in spirit with Christ Jesus and get *completely* involved with his mission of redeeming mankind.

To be truly Christian is to be co-missioned by Christ. To be baptized is to be immersed in his death and resurrection. To love Christ is to be one with Christ, to be like Christ, to live like him and die like him. His early followers were so convinced of this that they rejoiced when they suffered because this meant they were like their Master. They actually longed to suffer and die as martyrs: they practiced self-denial, fasting, and do-ing penance in order to die to self and to be ready to suffer with him whenever the op-portunity presented itself. Jesus asks us to take up our crosses daily and he will be ever faithful in seeing that each day has its crosses. We don't have to search for the cross. Our daily lives and daily duties provide our daily crosses.

To live like Christ and to die like Christ is to become like Christ: to pray for our per-secutors, to forgive those who have injured us, seventy times seven times if need be, to turn the other cheek, to walk the extra mile, to desire the best for all the rest because they too are children of our heavenly Father. Living like Christ means being possessed so thoroughly by Jesus that in a very real sense it is he who thinks and wills within us and who uses our bodies to act outside of us to bring his love to mankind, regardless of the cost. To live like Christ and to die like Christ is to realize that we cannot run when our hour to suffer comes; and it will come in small ways and in big ways many times in life.

Our own suffering makes real to us what Christ suffered for us. Our holy weeks of suffering and death will not make any more sense than the one Christ went through unless we understand "why," which is rooted in the mystery of love. "For God so loved the world that he gave his only Son" (John 3:16). The cross is still foolishness to the Greek and a stumbling block to the Jews. We don't have to dissect and analyze every bit of suffering that comes our way but we should try to accept it and understand that we are the part of the Body that needs to make up what is lacking in the suffering of Christ. And it is very important to realize that *the only thing lacking in Christ's suffering is our own participation in it.* We share in the redemptive suffering of Christ, as Pope John Paul II succinctly states:

> One can say that with the passion of Christ all human suffering has found itself in a new situation. And it is as though Job had foreseen this when he said: "I know that my Redeemer lives. . . ," and as though he had directed towards it his own suffering, which without the Redemption could not have revealed to him the fullness of its meaning. In the cross of Christ not only is the Redemption accomplished through suffering, but *also human suffering itself has been redeemed.* Christ—without any fault of His own—took on Himself "the total evil of sin." The experience of this evil determined the incomparable extent of Christ's suffering, which became *the price of the Redemption.* The Song of the Suffering Servant in Isaiah speaks of this.

In later times, the witnesses of the New Covenant, sealed in the Blood of Christ, will speak of this. These are the words of the Apostle Peter in his first letter: "You know that you were ransomed from the futile ways inherited from your fathers, not with perishable things such as silver or gold, but *with the precious blood of Christ,* like that of a lamb without blemish or spot." And the Apostle Paul in the letter to the Galatians will say: "He gave himself for our sins to deliver us from the present evil age," and in the first letter to the Corinthians: "You were bought with a price. So glorify God in your body."

With these and similar words the witnesses of the New Covenant speak of the greatness of the Redemption, accomplished through the suffering of Christ. The Redeemer suffered in place of man and for man. Every man has *his own share in the Redemption.* Each one is also *called to share in that suffering* through which the Redemption was accomplished. He is called to share in that suffering through which all human suffering has also been redeemed. In bringing about the Redemption through suffering, Christ *has* also *raised human suffering to the level of the Redemption.* Thus each man, in his suffering, can also become a sharer in the redemptive suffering of Christ.[2]

St. Peter tells us who we are:

> But you are a chosen race, a royal priesthood, a holy nation, God's own people, that you may declare the wonderful deeds of him who called you out of darkness into his marvelous light. Once you were no people but now you are God's people; once you had not received mercy but now you have received mercy. (1 Peter 2:9–10)

Jesus yearns for us to be one with him so that he can, through us, continually glorify

his Father. As a royal priesthood it is good
for us from time to time to meditate on the
prayer of the Mass—to ponder and reflect
upon it so that the spirit of these words can
draw us deeper and deeper into complete
participation in this holy, sacrificial action
of Jesus as well as of ourselves, if done prop-
erly.

The following are excerpts from the
Third Eucharistic Prayer of the Mass which
emphasize the sacrifice which Christ still
makes today in the Mass and the sacrifice
which he invites us to make also with him:

> From age to age you gather a people
> to yourself, so that from east to west
> a *perfect offering* may be made to the
> glory of your name. . . .

> Take this, all of you, and eat it: this
> is my body which *will be given up
> for you.* . . .

> Take this, all of you, and drink from
> it: this is the cup of my blood, the
> blood of the new and everlasting cov-

enant. *It will be shed for you and for all* so that sins may be forgiven. *Do this in memory of me. . . .*

Lord, by your *cross* and resurrection you have set us free. You are the Savior of the world.

Father, calling to mind *the death your Son endured* for our salvation, his glorious resurrection and ascension into heaven, and ready to greet him when he comes again, *we offer you in thanksgiving this holy and living sacrifice.* Look with favor on your Church's *offering, and see the Victim whose death* has reconciled us to yourself. . . .

May he make us an everlasting gift to you and enable us to share in the inheritance of your saints. . . .

Lord, may *this sacrifice*, which has made our peace with you, advance the peace and salvation of all the world.[3] (Emphasis added throughout)

The Mass is a reminder to us of the suffering of Jesus. In the Mass we celebrate the sacrifice he made to remain with us in the Eucharist. He becomes our nourishment, strengthening us to carry our daily crosses as an offering for the salvation of mankind.

5

God's Mercy

Jesus offers himself to the Father to release God's mercy on mankind: "In the days of his flesh, Jesus offered up prayers and supplications, with loud cries and tears, to him who was able to save him from death, and he was heard for his godly fear. Although he was a Son, he learned obedience through what he suffered; and being made perfect he became the source of eternal salvation to all who obey him" (Hebrews 5:7–9).

The Holy Sacrifice of the Mass, as we stated before, is Jesus' offering made present for us here and now. Offering ourselves along with Jesus to the Father here and now keeps God's mercy flowing. God gave us a way of continuing throughout the day our offering of the Holy Sacrifice of the Mass. He did this through a special prayer, called the Chaplet of Mercy, that Jesus gave to Blessed Sister Faustina Kowalska, a Polish sister who died in 1938. In the Eucharist we offer ourselves with Jesus to the Father in atonement for our sins and the sins of the whole world. The Chaplet of Divine Mercy keeps this offering ever before the mind. What great joy we should have in offering each day the Holy Sacrifice of the Mass and then continuing that offering throughout the day through use of the Chaplet.

The following relates the history of the Divine Mercy Chaplet and explains how to say it:

In 1933, God gave Sister Faustina a striking vision of His Mercy. Sister tells us: *"I saw a great light, with God the Father in the midst of it. Between this light and the earth I saw Jesus nailed to the Cross and in such a way that God, wanting to look upon the earth, had to look through Our Lord's wounds. And I understood that God blessed the earth for the sake of Jesus."* Of another vision on September 13, 1935, she writes: *"I saw an Angel, the executor of God's wrath . . .*

about to strike the earth. . . . I began to beg God earnestly for the world with words which I heard interiorly. As I prayed in this way, I saw the Angel's helplessness, and he could not carry out the just punishment. . . ."

The following day an inner voice taught her to say this prayer on ordinary rosary beads:

"First say one 'Our Father,' 'Hail Mary' *and* 'I believe.'

Then on the large beads say the following words:

'Eternal Father, I offer You the Body and Blood, Soul and Divinity of Your dearly beloved Son, Our Lord Jesus Christ, in atonement for our sins and those of the whole world.'

On the smaller beads you are to say the following words:

'For the sake of His sorrowful Passion have mercy on us and on the whole world.'

In conclusion you are to say these words three times:

'Holy God, Holy Mighty One, Holy Immortal One, have mercy on us and on the whole world.'"

Jesus said later to Sister Faustina: "Say unceasingly this chaplet that I have taught you. Anyone who says it will receive great Mercy at the hour of death. Priests will recommend it to sinners as the last hope. Even the most hardened sinner, if he recites this Chaplet even once, will receive grace from My infinite Mercy. I want the whole world to know My infinite Mercy. I want to give unimaginable graces to those who trust in My Mercy."[4]

The Divine Mercy Chaplet can be thought of as a "mini-Mass." It can be said day and night. It is one of the prayers I use to help me try to live in God's presence and to pray always, or to pray at every opportunity as St. Paul advises us to do. I pray it especially when I am making a spiritual sacrifice or working through pain, trials, and the like. I find it to be the most effective prayer for the sick and the dying and in times of special need. I really cannot begin to tell you how much it has done for my spiritual life. It keeps the Mass alive and present to me all day because we know that the Eucharist is actually being offered to God at every moment of the day and I use this prayer to participate in those offerings continuously.

I believe that the greatest action a Christian can take is to offer his humble self along with the Body and Blood, Soul and Divinity of our Lord Jesus Christ, in the Holy Spirit, to God the Father for the atonement of sin. This really is what is meant by "Greater love has no man than this, that a man lay down his life for his friends" (John 15:13).

6

Suffering Is Difficult

It is not easy to participate in the suffering of Christ. It was not easy for Jesus: "Father, if thou art willing, remove this cup from me; nevertheless not my will, but thine, be done" (Luke 22:42). It was not easy for his mother Mary or his disciples and it will not be easy for us.

I have a few small things that help me through difficult times and I want to share a few of them with you so you may add them to your own personal list.

There was once a king who felt he needed a ring that would help him to become more emotionally stable. He called in several wise men and told them that he wanted a ring that would make him happy when he was sad and sad when he was happy. After intense consultation the wise men presented him with a ring that simply read: "This too will pass." Knowing "this too will pass," both in our sadness and in our joy, will enable us to persevere in faithfulness.

Another one-liner that has helped me tremendously comes from Kipling's poem *If:* "If you can meet with Triumph and Disaster and treat both impostors the same. . . ." How many times our disasters are just exactly what we need to make us strong, to purify and sanctify us. How many times our triumphs lead us to pride and arrogance. This is the discipline of the cross.

This last one-liner helps me the most in times of difficulties:

Rejoice in the Lord always; again I will say, Rejoice. Let all men know your forbearance. The Lord is at hand. Have no anxiety about anything, but in everything by prayer and supplication with thanksgiving let your requests be made known to God. And the peace of God, which passes all understanding, will keep your hearts and your minds in Christ Jesus.

Finally, brethren, whatever is true, whatever is pure, whatever is lovely, whatever is gracious, if there is any excellence, if there is anything worthy of praise, think about these things. What you have learned and received and heard and seen in me, do; and the God of peace will be with you. (Philippians 4:4–9)

It is not sufficient simply to read this. We have to live these words. We must put them into practice, step by step, for them to bear fruit and help us in our need. Try this approach:

1) "Rejoice in the Lord always; again I will say, Rejoice." You can begin rejoicing right away because God intends this difficulty for your own good too!

2) "Let all men know your forbearance." You have a problem and you are rejoicing. This means you are unselfish and forbearing. You would not be rejoicing if you were selfish. Why are you rejoicing? Because "The Lord is at hand."

3) This is an important line: "Have no anxiety about anything." This is a command.

Send your anxiety and your fear on its way. In the name of Jesus, I command you, fear and anxiety, get out of my life!

4) Now, "in everything by prayer and supplication with thanksgiving let your requests be made known to God." Pray for your needs as well as the courage and perseverance to help you through your problems.

5) How good God is: "And the peace of God, which passes all understanding, will keep your hearts and your minds in Christ Jesus."

6) Now that the peace of God has returned, it is time to get on with your Christian walk: "Finally, brethren, whatever is true, whatever is pure, whatever is lovely, whatever is gracious, if there is any excellence, if there is anything worthy of praise, think about these things. What you have learned and received and heard and seen in me, do; and the God of peace will be with you." First, it is the peace of God that is standing guard over your hearts and minds, but after you begin to think correctly and do all that you

know you ought to do, it is the God of peace that is within you. As St. Paul said, "I have been crucified with Christ; it is no longer I who live, but Christ who lives in me" (Galatians 2:20). Put your heart into it. "And you shall love the Lord your God with all your heart, and with all your soul, and with all your might" (Deuteronomy 6:5).

7

In Praise of Suffering

There are many things in life which we do not understand, but that does not stop us from benefiting from them. I do not know any more about how a television works now than I did when I was a little boy. It was like science fiction to me then and it is like science fiction to me now. Yet with all my lack of understanding of television, I do not hesitate to turn it on upon those rare occasions when I think there is something of value to watch. The workings of the radio are likewise a mystery to me. The same goes for the telephone and the fax machine, but I still use them. Incidentally, I haven't even taken the time to find out what "fax" means. When it comes to the inner workings of computers, I am completely baffled. But I use them.

Similarly, we do not know all that we would like to know about suffering, but God through his revelation and through our own life experiences has made it clear that suffering is connected to his will and can have consequences of immense value. We can learn from the Book of Wisdom:

> The souls of the righteous are in the hand of God, and no torment will touch them. In the eyes of the foolish they seem to have died, and their departure was thought to be an affliction, and their going from us to be their destruction; but they are at peace. For though in the sight of men they were punished, their hope is full of immortality. Having been disciplined a little, they will receive great good, because God tested them and found them worthy of himself; like gold in the furnace he tried them, and like a sacrificial burnt offering he accepted them. In the time of their visitation they will shine forth, and will run like sparks through the stubble. They will govern nations and rule over peoples, and the Lord will reign over them for ever. Those who

trust in him will understand truth, and the faithful will abide with him in love, because grace and mercy are upon his elect, and he watches over his holy ones. (Wisdom 3:1–9)

St. Paul sheds light on the value of suffering in the following passage from Romans:

More than that, we rejoice in our sufferings, knowing that suffering produces endurance, and endurance produces character, and character produces hope, and hope does not disappoint us, because God's love has been poured into our hearts through the Holy Spirit who has been given to us.

While we were yet helpless, at the right time Christ died for the ungodly. Why, one will hardly die for a righteous man—though perhaps for a good man one will dare even to die. But God shows his love for us in that while we were yet sinners Christ died for us. (Romans 5:3–8)

We pray so many times for God to take away our sufferings, and there is nothing wrong with that. Yet we need to pray more for the grace to endure sufferings that can't be eased so that we can make up what is lacking in the Church.

St. Paul said: "May I never boast except in the cross of our Lord Jesus Christ" (Galatians 6:14 NABrNT). And when Paul presented his credentials to prove that he was an Apostle, he simply gave a list of his sufferings.

I am very aware in my own life, as well as in the lives of many people whom I know, that suffering and difficulties of many kinds have always left me somewhat wiser and stronger, for "we know that in everything God works for good with those who love him" (Romans 8:28).

Since so much good comes from suffering and pain, maybe it is time for us to stop being so negative about it. In real life circumstances we have coaches or those who encourage us as we go through difficult times. We need encouragement on our way to reaching the goals that lie before us, whether it be winning a championship, making it through school, learning how to play a musical instrument, or persevering in our work. Even our mothers had coaches to help them bring us into the world. God and his many followers can be our coaches, forever encouraging us by showing us the role that suffering is to play in our own personal salvation and that of the whole world. Jesus simply tells us that if we do not take up our crosses daily and follow him we cannot be his disciples. As Jesus said to James and John, "The cup that I drink you will drink; and with the baptism with which I am baptized, you will be baptized" (Mark 10:39). This is his way of encouraging us to follow him to the glorious kingdom of heaven. Jesus is *the Way*. *The Way* is the way of the cross that takes us by way of Calvary to the joy of the resurrection.

Once when Jesus was telling his disciples about his death and resurrection, Peter told our Lord that he would not let that happen. I think Jesus was looking for encouragement and support. Jesus rebuked Peter by saying, "Get behind me, Satan!" (Mark 8:33). I like to believe the Lord was saying to Peter, "Get behind me, don't block me; back me up, support me, help me to do what I have to do, for it is my Father's will that I suffer and die for my brothers and sisters."

I see Jesus' mother Mary playing the role of supporter by encouraging her Son to continue his Father's work. I have a sense that the Blessed Mother was quite aware of the woman in 2 Maccabees who encouraged each one of her seven sons to suffer and die at the hands of Antiochus' torturers rather than disobey God. I visualize Mary playing an important role at the foot of the cross. I see Jesus drawing strength from his mother as he saw her being faithful unto his death, even death on the cross.

To encourage is to give courage to a person so he can persevere, that is, continue doing that which is severe or difficult. We all need courage and we need others to stand by us. I have a homespun definition of courage

I would like to share with you. We Italians use the word "courage" often. *"Cour"* means heart; add the word "age" to it to mean an aged, mature heart—one that is able to handle pain and suffering. I also like to say that courage means putting a little rage into your heart.

St. Francis of Assisi, the founder of the Franciscan family, loved life and God's creation so much that he left us a bit of prose called *The Canticle of Brother Sun.* He considered all of God's creatures his brothers and sisters. He even considers death his sister as seen in the stanza below:

> Praised be you, my Lord, for our
> Sister Bodily Death
> From whom no living man can
> escape.
> Woe to those who die in mortal sin.
> Blessed are those whom death will
> find in your most holy will,
> For the second death shall do them
> no harm.[5]

Francis called death his sister because he knew that death opened the door to Eternal

Life. I believe that we should also honor suffering because we know and believe that it plays a major role in our salvation. We could say something like:

Praised be you, my Lord, for
Brother Suffering,
That purifies us and makes us holy
By uniting us to the suffering of the crucified One,
and makes us sharers in His
redeeming action.

I have one more thought I would like to share before closing this chapter in praise of suffering, written on the feast of All Souls. I was thinking about what would happen if I were to die before carrying out all of God's plans for me. What if God's plan were for me to preach 3,000 homilies during my lifetime but I had preached only 2,800? There would be no place for me to preach the remaining 200. If I were to have celebrated 5,000 sacraments of reconciliation and missed that number by 500, it would just have to end that way.

Yet, surprisingly, if I should die without reaching my quota of suffering, God will have a place for me to finish the suffering that I have not endured on earth. We Catholics call that place purgatory, i.e., a place where suffering continues its work of purifying us. Imagine that! Suffering is so important there is even a special place where we have to make it up after death.

We need to see the value of suffering in our own purification. But more than that we need to understand that our suffering, along with Jesus', helps to redeem those brothers and sisters who still need redemption. I recommend we call suffering Brother Suffering and I believe, as St. Paul taught, we should rejoice in our sufferings because they are important ingredients in God's plan of building his everlasting kingdom. As St. Peter said:

> But rejoice to the extent that you share in the sufferings of Christ, so that when his glory is revealed you may also rejoice exultantly. If you are

insulted for the name of Christ, blessed are you, for the Spirit of glory and of God rests upon you. (1 Peter 4:13–14 NABrNT)

As Jesus said: "Greater love has no man than this, that a man lay down his life for his friends" (John 15:13).

8

Our Lady of Fatima and Our Lady's Apparitions

In the messages of our Lady of Fatima, the importance of our acts of redemptive suffering, reparation, penance, and the offering of all things to God in atonement for sin are very clearly stated from the beginning to the end. During the first apparition our Lady asked the children:

> "Do you want to offer yourselves to God to bear all the sufferings which He wants to send you, as an act of reparation for the sins which offend Him and as pleas for the conversion of sinners?"

> "Yes, we do."

> "You will have a lot to suffer then, but God's grace will be your comfort."[6]

Our Lady also said: "Sacrifice yourselves for sinners and say often, especially whenever you make a sacrifice: 'O my Jesus, it is for love of Thee, in reparation for the offenses committed against the Immaculate Heart of Mary, and for the conversion of poor sinners.'"[7]

And she taught them to pray after each mystery of the rosary: "O my Jesus forgive us; save us from the fire of Hell; take all souls to heaven, especially those most in need."[8]

The following is a prayer that the angel at Fatima gave to the children for their use and ours:

O Most Holy Trinity, Father, Son and Holy Spirit, I adore Thee profoundly and I offer Thee the Most Precious Body, Blood, Soul and Divinity of Jesus Christ, present in all the Tabernacles of the world, in reparation for the outrages, sacrileges and indifference by which He is offended.

By the infinite merits of the Sacred Heart of Jesus, and the Immaculate Heart of Mary, I beg the conversion of poor sinners.[9]

Our Lady of Lourdes, during her seventh apparition, simply said, "Penance, Penance, Penance!"

St. Bernadette of Lourdes said, "My job is being sick."[10]

Beginning in the spring of 1947, our Lady reportedly appeared for many years as the "Rosa Mystica" or Mystical Rose in Montichiari-Fontanelle, Italy. I believe her message is highly relevant to our topic of redemptive suffering.

During one of the earliest apparitions to Pierina Gilli, a nurse in the local hospital, she appeared with three large swords in her heart. She gave the meaning of the symbols as follows: The first sword means the loss of vocations for priests or monks. The second sword means priests, monks, and nuns who live in deadly sin. The third sword means priests and monks who commit the treason of Judas. While giving up their vocation, they also often lose their faith, their eternal beatitude, and become enemies of the Church.

To combat these problems, our Lady asked for "prayer, sacrifice, and penance" from her children and showed three colored roses as symbols of them doing those actions. She explained that the white rose was the spirit of prayer, the red rose the spirit of expiation and sacrifice, and the yellow rose the spirit of penitence. She said that penitence means the acceptance of the little daily crosses we are given and also doing one's work in the spirit of penitence.[11]

9

Saints of God

As we look at the lives of the saints, we notice that, in one way or another, they all were victims with Christ Jesus, the Lamb of God who takes away the sin of the world. I have chosen to mention a few of the many saints who have touched my life because of the way they participated in redemptive suffering.

The way the death of **St. Stephen**, the first martyr, is recorded in the Acts of the Apostles has always been a source of inspiration to me.

> Now when they heard these things they were enraged, and they ground their teeth against him. But he, full of the Holy Spirit, gazed into heaven and saw the glory of God, and Jesus standing at the right hand of God; and he said, "Behold, I see the heavens opened, and the Son of man

standing at the right hand of God."
But they cried out with a loud voice
and stopped their ears and rushed together upon him. Then they cast him
out of the city and stoned him; and
the witnesses laid down their gar-
ments at the feet of a young man
named Saul. And as they were ston-
ing Stephen, he prayed, "Lord Jesus,
receive my spirit." And he knelt down
and cried with a loud voice, "Lord,
do not hold this sin against them."
And when he had said this, he fell
asleep. (Acts 7:54–60)

Jesus told the apostles to pray for their
persecutors. Jesus himself prayed for his per-
secutors when he was on the cross. Dismas
the thief and Longinus the centurion were
converted. Stephen prayed for his persecutors. Could this have contributed to St. Paul's
conversion? Our God has not changed. Praying for our persecutors can mean Eternal Life
for them.

Blessed Sister Faustina, who died in Poland in 1938 at the age of 33, was used by

God to promote the devotion to Divine
Mercy. She is a perfect example of how far
we can go to participate in the redemptive
suffering of Christ. The following, taken
from the diary of Blessed Faustina, is used
in the liturgy on her feast day, October 5:

> Make of me, Jesus, a pure and
> agreeable offering before the Face of
> Your Father. Jesus, transform me,
> miserable and sinful as I am, into
> Your own self (for You can do all
> things), and give me to Your Eternal
> Father. I want to become a sacrificial
> host before you, but an ordinary wa-
> fer to people. I want the fragrance of
> my sacrifice to be known to You
> alone.[12]

Our Lord encapsulated the essence of redemptive suffering in these statements made
to Sister Faustina in a talk entitled *Confer-
ence on Sacrifice and Prayer*:

> "My daughter, I want to instruct
> you on how you are to rescue souls
> through sacrifice and prayer. You will

save more souls through prayer and suffering than will a missionary through his teachings and sermons alone. I want to see you as a sacrifice of living love, which only then carries weight before Me. You must be annihilated, destroyed, living as if you were dead in the most secret depths of your being. You must be destroyed in that secret depth where the human eye has never penetrated; then will I find in you a pleasing sacrifice, a holocaust full of sweetness and fragrance. And great will be your power for whomever you intercede. Outwardly, your sacrifice must look like this: silent, hidden, permeated with love, imbued with prayer. I demand, My daughter, that your sacrifice be pure and full of humility, that I may find pleasure in it. I will not spare My grace, that you may be able to fulfill what I demand of you.

"I will now instruct you on what your holocaust shall consist of, in everyday life, so as to preserve you from illusions. You shall accept all sufferings with love. Do not be afflicted if your heart often experiences repugnance and dislike for sacrifice. All its power rests in the will, and so these contrary feelings, far from lowering the value of the sacrifice in My eyes, will enhance it. Know that your body and soul will often be in the midst of fire. Although you will not feel My presence on some occasions, I will always be with you. Do not fear; My grace will be with you. . . ."[13]

Saint Margaret Mary Alaquoque (1647-1690), whom God used to promote the Sacred Heart devotion, wrote much about suffering with Christ. Jesus asked her to rise from sleep every Thursday night between 11 p.m. and midnight and to spend an hour prostrate before the Blessed Sacrament meditating on his agony in the garden of Gethsemane. On the value of suffering she wrote thus:

> I know of no other happiness in life than to remain ever hidden in our

62

nothingness—to suffer and love in silence—to embrace our crosses, prais-
ing and thanking Him Who gives
them to us. (II, 258)

Suffer bravely, and be content
that the divine good pleasure be accomplished in you. You must ever be
immolated and sacrificed to it with
unshaken trust that the Sacred Heart
will not forsake you. It is closer to
you in suffering than in consolation.
(II, 700)[14]

Blessed Margaret of Costello lived in
Italy in the fourteenth century.

. . . Margaret was grossly de-
formed. She was ugly, a midget, a
hunchback, totally blind, so lame that
she could hardly walk. Ashamed of
her, her rich parents locked her up for
years. Finally, they deliberately lost
her in a distant city. . . . She never
became bitter, never complained,
never reproached others or lost heart.
. . . Margaret was courageous because

she looked at suffering with the eyes of faith. She did not know why God permitted her to have so many afflictions. She did know that He was an infinitely loving and kind Father, who never permits one single misfortune without good reason, who always turns evil into good for His children.

She wondered why people pitied her. Was it not a privilege to suffer with Christ? Suffering for her was a way to heaven. Pain made Margaret sympathetic and understanding toward others.[15]

Like many others who desire to emulate the sufferings of Jesus, she died at the age of thirty-three.

Another favorite of mine is **Blessed Elizabeth of the Trinity** (1880–1906). *Elizabeth* means "house of God": Father, Son, and Holy Spirit. God used her to promote the mystery of the indwelling of the Father, Son, and Holy Spirit in the Christian soul.

Elizabeth once said, "It seems to me that I have found my heaven on earth, for heaven is God and God is in my soul. On the day I understood that, everything became clear to me. . . ."[16]

During Blessed Elizabeth of the Trinity's last retreat she wrote, referring thus to herself:

Then, when her hour of humiliation, of annihilation comes, she will recall this little phrase, "Jesus autem tacebat" [Jesus was silent]; and she will be silent, "keeping all her strength for the Lord"; this strength which "we draw from silence." And when the hour of abandonment, of desertion, and of anguish comes, the hour that drew from Christ this loud cry, "Why have You abandoned Me?" she will recall this prayer: "that they may have in themselves the fulness of My joy"; and drinking to the dregs "the cup prepared by the Father," she will find a divine sweetness in its bitterness. Finally, after having said so often "I am thirsty," thirsty to possess You in glory, she will sing: "Everything is consummated; into Your hands I commend my spirit." And the Father will come for her to "bring her into His inheritance," where in "the light she will see light."

"Know that the Lord has marvelously glorified his Holy One," David sang. Yes, the Holy One of God will have been glorified in this soul, for He will have destroyed everything there to "clothe it with Himself," and it will have lived in reality the words of the Precursor: "He must increase and I must decrease."[17]

Saint John Vianney (1786-1859), the Curé of Ars, is also a beautiful example for the soul willing to suffer for the Lord. The following quotes are taken from *Thoughts of the Curé D'Ars:*[18]

We have nothing of our own but our will. It is the only thing which God has so placed in our own power that we can make an offering of it to him.

Oh! How I love those words said the first thing in the morning: I will do and suffer everything this day for the Glory of God . . . nothing for the world or personal interest, all to please my Saviour!

There are people who make capital out of everything, even the winter. If it is cold, they offer their little sufferings to God.

In your work, offer your difficulties and troubles quite simply to God . . . and you will find that his blessing will rest upon you and all you do.

Sister Josefa Menendez (1890–1923) lived in Poitiers, France, as a sister of the Society of the Sacred Heart. The other sisters knew her only as a good religious.

Josefa's superiors, however, knew that from her postulancy Josefa had received frequent mystical visits from the Sacred Heart, who had chosen her to be a victim of His justice and mercy and to spread the message of His boundless love for souls. . . .

Our Lord showed Josefa that her mission was to suffer much to console His Heart and save souls from Hell. . . .

Explaining the value of this way of life, He said to her, "It is I who allow the souls I love to suffer. Suffering is necessary for all, but how much more for My chosen souls! . . . It purifies them, and I am thus able to make use of them to snatch many from hell fire.". . .

. . . Our Lady also explained Jesus' plans to use Josefa as His messenger: "Jesus wishes His words to remain hidden as long as you live. After your death, they will be known from one end of the earth to the other, and in their light many souls will be saved through confidence and abandonment to the merciful Heart of Jesus.". . .

Our Lord said to Josefa . . . "Nothing great is required, the smallest acts suffice: a step taken, a straw picked up, a glance restrained, a service rendered, a cordial smile . . . all these offered to Love are in reality of great profit to souls and draw down floods of grace on them."[19]

The following quote is taken from *The Way of Divine Love* which contains numerous quotes from Sister Menendez's own writings. Our Lady said to her:

When you suffer, it is Jesus who reposes in you, so what is there to fear? Abandon yourself to His will. You cannot imagine now what your joy will be for all eternity in heaven, when you see the many souls saved by your little acts and sacrifices. Life is of no account, and yours will pass like a flash! Use every moment of it to merit, by giving your heavenly Bridegroom the glory of complete surrender to His good pleasure. Live in His peace and love, and above all leave Him free to use you.[20]

Saint Maximilian Kolbe, a great saint of our age, is known throughout the world because he literally laid down his life for another. Maximilian was a Nazi prisoner during the Second World War in the concentration camp of Auschwitz, the German name for the town of Oswiecim, Poland. One morning the Nazis were choosing ten men to be put to death by starvation as a means of punishment of the camp because one prisoner had escaped. Francis Gajowniczek was one of the men singled out. He broke down, crying out, "my wife and my children." Fr. Maximilian Kolbe offered to die in his place and his request was granted. For two weeks, Fr. Kolbe led those being starved in the rosary, hymns, and devotions. Their prayers were overheard by the other prisoners.

His heroic actions were the result of a lifetime of preparation. The following words were taken from talks he gave to his Franciscan brothers during the beginning of the Nazi persecution:

During the first three centuries, the Church was persecuted. The blood of martyrs watered the seeds of Christianity. Later, when the persecutions ceased, one of the Fathers of the Church deplored the lukewarmness of Christians. He rejoiced when persecutions returned. In the same way, we must rejoice in what will happen, for in the midst of trials our zeal will become more ardent. Besides, are we not in the hands of the Blessed Virgin? Is it not our most ardently desired ideal to give our lives for her? We live only once. We die only once. Therefore let it be according to her good pleasure.

Once war came, he did not change his tune:

"God is cleansing Poland," he said. "After this her [spiritual] light will shine on the world."

and

We are living in a time of intense penance. Let us at least avail ourselves of it. Suffering is a good and sweet thing for him who accepts it wholeheartedly.[21]

He spoke to them "on the three stages of life: first stage, the preparation for activity; the second, activity itself; third, suffering.

The third stage of life, the one of suffering, I think will be my lot shortly. But by whom, where, how, and in what form this suffering will come is still unknown. However, I'd like to suffer and die in a knightly manner, even to the shedding of the last drop of my blood in order to hasten the day of gaining the whole world for God through the Immaculate Mother. I wish the same for you as for myself. What nobler thing can I wish you, my dear sons? If I knew something better, I'd wish it for you, but I don't. According to St. John [15:13] Christ Himself said, "Greater

love than this no one has, than to lay
down his life for his friends."[22]

These words of St. Maximilian Kolbe,
so important to a world that had yet to suffer
through the devastating Second World War,
may be just as important to the world of chaos
in which we now live.

I truly believe, deep in my spirit, that the
world's present condition is much worse than
it was in 1938 and that it is going to get even
worse before it gets better. I also believe that
there is more suffering now than ever before
and that it is going to get more intense before it is alleviated completely. How important it is for us to understand the value of
suffering so that we can accept the portion
that belongs to us. It is only by doing so that
we can unite our sufferings with the suffering of Christ, thus making it redemptive suffering.

I would like to give you an account of
the stigmata of **St. Francis of Assisi**, the
founder of the Third Order Regular of Penance of which I am very happy to be a mem-

ber. St. Francis, who died in 1226, lived a very disciplined, ascetical, and penitential life; a life of ongoing conversion. His last few years were extremely difficult. He experienced physical sufferings, since he had worn himself out in the service of Christ, as well as moral sufferings as he saw many of his followers no longer adhering to his idea of living in utter poverty for the Kingdom of God. This can be considered the final step in the stripping of St. Francis so that he could be identified with Christ, the Crucified One. The stigmata itself can be considered an external sign of what had already taken place interiorly. May the following words speak to your heart:

"The Stigmata of St. Francis" from St. Bonaventure's *Major Life of Francis:*

> St. Francis . . . had learned how to distribute the time in which he could gain merit wisely, devoting part of it to his neighbor by doing good, and part to the restful ecstasy of contemplation. According to the demands of time or circumstances he would

devote himself wholly to the salvation of his neighbor, but when he finished, he would escape from the distracting crowds and go into solitude in search of peace. There he was free to attend exclusively to God and he would cleanse any stain he had contracted while living in the midst of the world.

Two years before his death . . . he began a forty-day fast in honor of St. Michael the Archangel, as was his custom, and he soon experienced an extraordinary in-pouring of divine contemplation. He was all on fire with heavenly desires and he realized that the gifts of divine grace were being poured out over him in greater abundance than ever. He was borne aloft not as one who would search curiously into the divine majesty and be crushed by its glory (cf. Prv 25, 27), but as a faithful and wise servant anxious only to discover God's will, which he wanted to obey with all his heart and soul. . . .

. . . Then one morning about the feast of the Exaltation of the Holy Cross, while he was praying on the mountainside, Francis saw a Seraph with six fiery wings coming down from the highest point in the heavens. The vision descended swiftly and came to rest in the air near him. Then he saw the image of a Man crucified in the midst of the wings, with his hands and feet stretched out and nailed to a cross. Two of the wings were raised above his head and two were stretched out in flight, while the remaining two shielded his body. Francis was dumbfounded at the sight and his heart was flooded with a mixture of joy and sorrow. . . .

. . . Eventually he realized by divine inspiration that God had shown him this vision in his providence, in order to let him see that, as Christ's lover, he would resemble Christ crucified perfectly not by physical martyrdom, but by the fervor of his spirit. As the vision disappeared, it left his heart ablaze with eagerness and impressed upon his body a miraculous likeness. There and then the marks of nails began to appear in his hands and feet, just as he had seen them in his vision of the Man nailed to the Cross. His hands and feet appeared pierced through the center with nails, the heads of which were in the palms of his hands and on the instep of each foot, while the points stuck out on the opposite side. The heads were black and round, but the points were long and bent back, as if they had been struck with a hammer; they rose above the surrounding flesh and stood out from it. His right side seemed as if it had been pierced with a lance and was marked with a livid scar which often bled, so that his habit and trousers were stained.[23]

The Testament Prayer of
St. Francis of Assisi:

We adore you, Lord Jesus Christ, in all your churches in the whole world, and we bless you, because by your holy cross you have redeemed the world.

The Prayer of St. Francis of Assisi
before His Crucifix:

All-highest, glorious God,
cast your light into the darkness
of my heart.
Give me right faith,
firm hope,
perfect charity
and profound humility,
with wisdom and perception,
O Lord, so that I may do
what is truly your holy will.
Amen.

10

I Am the Resurrection and the Life

After saying all this we must conclude that death is not our goal; it is the way to our goal of the resurrection and ascension into glory. Each time we pray the Angelus we are reminded of this.

> Pour forth, we beseech You, O Lord, Your grace into our hearts, that we to whom the Incarnation of Christ, Your Son, was made known by the message of an angel, may by His passion and Cross be brought to the glory of His Resurrection, through the same Christ, our Lord. Amen.[24]

St. Paul, who is the best teacher on death, is also an excellent teacher of the resurrection. He begins by telling us that we get the grace to suffer and die from the resurrection itself.

I wish to know Christ and the power flowing from his resurrection; likewise to know how to share in his sufferings by being formed into the pattern of his death. Thus do I hope that I may arrive at resurrection from the dead. . . .

. . . My entire attention is on the finish line as I run toward the prize to which God calls me—life on high in Christ Jesus. All of us who are spiritually mature must have this attitude. If you see it another way, God will clarify the difficulty for you. It is important that we continue on our course, no matter what stage we have reached. (Phillipians 3:10–12, 14–16 NAB)

My brothers and sisters, during our journey through the "dark valley" (Psalm 23:4), we must keep our eyes fixed on the resurrection and Christ Jesus glorified if we are going to rejoice in the sufferings of Christ as well as our own sufferings. Our hope and our joy flow from the resurrected, glorified Christ.

We don't know everything about the resurrection but we know enough. Our Lord tells us that unless we imitate the seed which goes into the ground and dies, we cannot have life. It is indeed a paradox that from death comes life, yet it should not be that hard to believe since we see it frequently in all of creation. St. Paul goes on to tell us that what comes out of the grave will be nothing like what we put into it. Just as the large oak tree comes from the acorn, so too our risen bodies will be unlike that corpse we plant.

Jesus was the first one to experience this most fascinating occurrence, which will be ours also one day. We talk about the joy of Jesus' followers when he arose. How about the joy of God the Father? How about the joy of Jesus who rose and the Holy Spirit who brought Jesus back from the dead? Jesus was raised from the dead as a totally new creation. Jesus was the firstborn of many. Before he died he had a physical body, but shortly thereafter he had a "spiritual body" (1 Corinthians 15:44), as St. Paul calls it, a completely new entity in God's creation.

What was put in the tomb was mortal, what came out was immortal. What went into the tomb was subject to the physical laws of our human condition, and what came forth was totally clothed with the supernatural.

My favorite image of this is the caterpillar that "dies" in order to become a butterfly. His crawling days are over: now he flies. To believe in the death and resurrection of Christ is to believe in the end of our crawling days and the beginning of our flying ones.

Jesus came to change the meaning of death. "Death" meant "end" until Jesus died. Jesus put Death to death. And he brought Life to life. St. Paul put it nicely: "O death, where is thy victory? O death, where is thy sting?" (1 Corinthians 15:55).

My brothers and sisters, our brother Jesus has truly risen from the dead and ascended into heaven. He now sits at the right hand of the Father constantly praying for us and preparing a place for us. He will not be satisfied until we all have new bodies just like his.

St. John's words are an inspiration to us that our end is really a new beginning:

> Then I saw a new heaven and a new earth; for the first heaven and the first earth had passed away, and the sea was no more. And I saw the holy city, new Jerusalem, coming down out of heaven from God, prepared as a bride adorned for her husband; and I heard a great voice from the throne saying, "Behold, the dwelling of God is with men. He will dwell with them, and they shall be his people, and God himself will be with them; he will wipe away every tear from their eyes, and death shall be no more, neither shall there be mourning nor crying nor pain any more, for the former things have passed away." (Revelation 21:1–4)

The Spirit and the Bride say "Come!" And let him who hears say, "Come." And let him who is thirsty come, let him who desires take the water of life without price.

He who testifies to these things says, "Surely I am coming soon." Amen. Come Lord Jesus! (Revelation 22:17, 20)

The day that I was to send this book to the publisher, my collaborators randomly chose, as part of their morning prayers, a reading from *To the Priests, Our Lady's Beloved Sons*, a book composed of interior locutions from our Blessed Mother to Father Stefano Gobbi, the head of the Marian Movement of Priests. To me, the reading is providential, so I share part of it with you as the conclusion to this booklet. The reading was given to Fr. Gobbi on Good Friday, March 24, 1989. The chapter is entitled "Remain with Jesus, on the Cross":

O sweet and saving wood, upon which is hung the price of our ransom! O Cross, blessed and sanctified by the Paschal Victim who today is immolating Himself upon you in the one and only Sacrifice which redeems and saves all!

Beloved sons, on this day of Good Friday, permit that I might repeat also to you: *Remain with Jesus, on the Cross.* Do not give in to the subtle temptations of my Adversary, to the facile seductions of the world, to the voices of those who again today repeat to you: "Come down from the Cross!"

No! You also, like Jesus, must understand the divine plan of your personal priestly offering. You too must say *yes* to the will of the Father and be open to words of prayer and of pardon. Because today, you also, like Jesus, must be immolated for the salvation of the world.[25]

11

Special Prayers

Prayer to the Blessed Sacrament

Prayed twice daily by Franciscan T.O.R.s*

V. We adore you, O Christ, here and in all your churches throughout the world, and bless you.

R. Because by your Holy Cross you have redeemed the world.

Antiphon. O Sacred Banquet, in which Christ is received, the memory of his Passion renewed, the mind is filled with grace, and a pledge of future glory is given to us.

V. You have given them bread from heaven.

R. Having all sweetness within it.

Let us pray

  O God, in this wondrous sacrament you have left us a memorial of your Passion. We ask you to enable us so to worship the sacred

* Third Order Regular of Penance

mysteries of your Body and Blood that we may constantly feel in our lives the effects of your redemption. You who live and reign for ever and ever. Amen.

Prayer to the Holy Spirit

Come Holy Spirit, fill the hearts of your faithful and kindle in them the fire of your love.

V. Send forth your Spirit, and they shall be created.

R. And you shall renew the face of the earth.

Let us pray

O God, who instructs the hearts of the faithful by the light of the Holy Spirit, grant that, by the gift of the same Spirit, we may be always truly wise, and ever rejoice in His consolation, through Christ our Lord. Amen.

Short Prayer of Commitment

Jesus, I repent of my sins.
I renounce the evil one and all his works.
I surrender my life to you and I truly accept
    you as the Son of the Living God.

I receive you now into my life as my personal Lord and Savior.

Fill me with your Holy Spirit. I love you, Jesus.[26]

Source Notes

[1]*Dominicae Cenae,* n. 9, *Origins,* March 27, 1980, vol. 9, no. 41, p. 659.

[2]*Salvifici Doloris,* n. 19, Vatican translation.

[3]*The Catholic Missal,* Eucharistic Prayer III.

[4]*Devotion to the Divine Mercy,* pamphlet (Stockbridge, MA: Marian Helpers, 1993).

[5]*Prayers of St. Francis of Assisi,* pamphlet, trans. R. Armstrong (Cincinnati: St. Anthony Messenger Press, 1979).

[6]Robert J. Fox, *Fatima Today* (Front Royal, VA: Christendom Publications, 1983), p. 20.

[7]Ibid., p. 23.

[8]Ibid., Appendix, p. 255.

[9]Ibid.

[10]Sr. Mary Francis LeBlanc, O.Carm., *Cause of Our Joy* (Boston: St. Paul Books and Media, 1991), p. 45.

[11] See *Maria Rosa Mystica* by A. M. Weigl.

[12] *Divine Mercy in My Soul: The Diary of the Servant of God, Sister M. Faustina Kowalska,* trans. G. W. Kosicki (Stockbridge, MA: Marian Press, 1987), p. 483.

[13] Ibid., pg. 1767.

[14] *Thoughts and Sayings of St. Margaret Mary for Every Day of the Year,* trans. Sisters of the Visitation Partridge Green (Rockford, IL: Tan Books and Publishers), pp. 81–82.

[15] Taken from a pamphlet from the Shrine of Blessed Margaret of Castello, Columbus, Ohio.

[16] Ann Ball, *Modern Saints: Their Lives and Faces,* Book Two (Rockford, IL: Tan Books and Publishers, 1983), p. 251.

[17] *Elizabeth of The Trinity, The Complete Works I,* trans. Aletheia Kane, O.C.D. (Washington: ICS Publications, 1984), pp. 159–160.

[18]*Thoughts of the Curé D'Ars,* comp. W. M. B. (Rockford, IL: Tan Books and Publishers, 1984), pp. 6–11.

[19]Ann Ball, *Modern Saints,* pp. 346, 348.

[20]*The Way of Divine Love or The Message of the Sacred Heart to the World: A Short Biography of His Messenger Sister Josefa Menéndez* (Westminster, MD: Newman Press, 1964), p. 404.

[21]Patricia Treece, *A Man For Others: Maximilian Kolbe, Saint of Auschwitz, in the Words of Those Who Knew Him* (San Francisco: Harper and Row, 1982), p. 107.

[22]Patricia Treece, *A Man For Others,* pp. 75–76.

[23]*St. Francis of Assisi: Writings and Early Biographies—English Omnibus of the Sources for the Life of St. Francis,* trans. R. Brown, B. Fahy, et al; ed. M. A. Habig (Chicago: Franciscan Herald Press, 1973), pp. 729–731.

[24]Fr. Michael Scanlan, T.O.R., and Fr. John P. Bertolucci, S.F.O., *Prayers and Blessings for Daily Life in Christ* (Steubenville, OH: Franciscan University Press, 1989, rev. ed), p. 48.

[25]*To the Priests, Our Lady's Beloved Sons* (St. Francis, ME: The Marian Movement of Priests, 1991), p. 636.

[26]Scanlan and Bertolucci, *Prayers and Blessings,* p. 13.

Acknowledgments

If I were to mention by name everyone who helped me write this book, you would be left wondering if any of it is mine.

I do, however, want to thank the Holy Spirit who I believe inspired me and all those who helped me.

I want to thank my families, both my relatives and my Franciscan family, who have been a constant support and have shown me, by their example, what redemptive suffering is all about.

I would like to thank all my friends who took the time to give me constructive criticism and all those who encouraged me by telling me to continue preaching on redemptive suffering and to write something on this important topic.

I extend special thanks to my friend and Franciscan brother Fr. Michael Scanlan, T.O.R., who supported me and took the time to write the foreword.

Thanks to my publisher, Franciscan University Press, its director and editors.

And finally, I would like to thank my friends Tom and Mickey Krebs for all of their collaborative efforts in the completion of *Redemptive Suffering*.